Copyright © 2023 Charlene Francis.

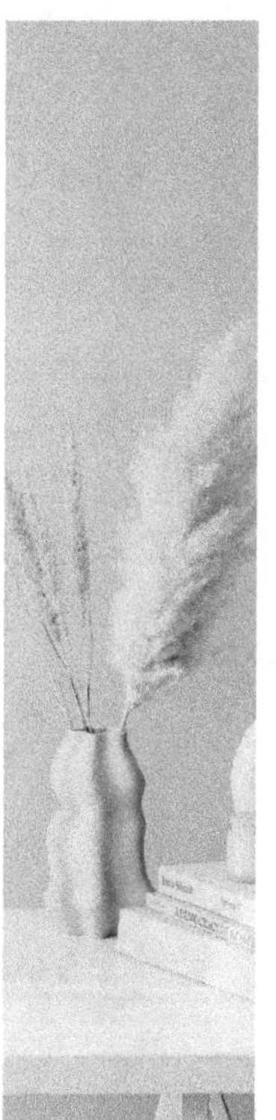

The events and conversations in this book have been set down to the best of the author's ability, although some names and details have been changed to protect the privacy of individuals.

The books mentioned by John Eckhardt.
1. Prayer That Rout Demons.
2. Prophet Arise.

Front cover image by Unknown Artist
Book design by Charlene Francis
First eBook edition 2023.

www.KingdomRestores.com

Table of Contents

Table of Contents

Chapter 1: Generational Curses

Before the wilderness, my life was shaped by generational curses. From the moment I was born, it seemed that no matter how talented or gifted I was, things would always be hard for me. But despite these challenges, I knew that Yah had a plan for me. I was still very much anointed, able to see and hear in the spirit, and had the gift of knowledge. At times, I could even tell others what God was saying to me about them.

However, along with these gifts came intense emotions. At times, I thought they were my own but later realized that I was feeling the people around me. It was overwhelming and scary, especially when I found myself in a hospital and was told in a dream that a lady was about to die. Waking up to her grieving family was a moment that will forever stay with me. It was sad, and I felt helpless.

Growing up, I spent a large amount of my youth and young adult life in the church. I experienced many forms of deliverance, but never once was I given guidance on how to break the deadly curses and covenants in my life. It was frustrating to see these generational curses visibly affecting my life, but not fully understanding how to break free from them.

Thankfully, Yahweh would one day bring me to His sources, where I could finally find the freedom I prayed for on many occasions. It was a journey, but with God's miracles, I was able to break free from the generational curses that had plagued my life for so long.

Chapter 2: Demonic Systems

Growing up in a broken home was tough, to say the least. My mother was a drug addict, and my father was somewhat absent, which left me feeling like I was missing out on something. I lived with my maternal grandmother, who worked two jobs to make ends meet for her five children and a few grandchildren. Despite the difficulties, my grandparents did their best to raise me, and I am forever grateful to them.

At school, I felt like I was treated differently because of my family situation. My teachers would often give me extra attention and try to help me with my problems, which made me feel like there was something wrong with me. Social services also entered my life, but they were not helpful at all, and I felt like they didn't care about my well-being. One incident that stands out in my mind is when I was targeted by the police because of a racist man's false accusation. My very white school friends knocked on his car window while he was asleep, and we all ran. The police arrested me even though I hadn't done anything wrong. While in the station, I felt helpless and afraid. I kept calling and asking to be let out of the cell, and it was a terrifying experience.

These attacks and micro-aggressions continued throughout my teenage and early adult years. I was often told that I was "very well-spoken" as if I should have been speaking slang to fit in with my black ghetto surroundings. It was frustrating and hurtful to be judged based on stereotypes and assumptions.

Despite all of this, I knew that Yahweh had a plan for my life. I had been anointed and had the gift of knowledge, which allowed me to see and hear in the spirit.

In the wilderness, I learned that I was not alone in my struggles and that others had similar experiences. I also learned that there were demonic systems at work in my life, trying to hold me back and keep me from fulfilling my purpose. Through prayer and spiritual warfare, I was able to break free and begin to live the life that Yahweh had intended for me.

Leaving home was a difficult decision, but I knew it was necessary. Living with my grandmother, aunt, uncles, cousins, and sometimes my mother was becoming too much to handle. The constant abuse and trauma were taking a toll on me, and I needed to break free from it all.

After leaving home, I found myself in emergency accommodation for the homeless and needy. It was a shared house, more like a hostel, and I had to leave my job at Harrods, the department store where I had worked and loved. But I was determined to find my freedom.

The first year of living on my own was tough. I was completely alone, and I had to learn to fend for myself. But despite the challenges, I managed to remain celibate, which was a big deal for me. My innocence had already been taken away at a young age, but I was determined not to let anyone else take it from me.

During this time, I realized that I needed guidance and support. I was lost and unsure of what to do next. But those around me seemed unwilling or unable to provide the tools I needed. So, I turned to Yahweh, and that's when my true journey began.

I found my way to baptism, and it was a turning point for me. I began to see myself differently, as someone worthy of love and respect. I realized that the abuse and trauma I had experienced didn't define me. I was more than my past, and I had the power to create a new future for myself.

Finding freedom in the wilderness was not easy, but it was necessary for my growth and healing. It was a time of self-discovery, where I learned to trust myself and my instincts. And although I still had a long way to go, I was on the right path, and nothing could stop me from achieving my goals.

Now that I had my place, I thought I had finally found my way to independence. However, life still had a way of throwing me curveballs. I was given a flat of a family member that had lost her place due to rent arrears. It was not intentional, but some would say it was a coincidence. Before that, while in temporary accommodation, I was given a place that belonged to a gran aunt before she died. All these spirits and occasions continued to follow me.

After getting baptized, which was an amazing experience, I thought I had finally found spiritual freedom. But before that, I had many attacks, which affected my mental health, my home, and my finances. It was as if I was under constant siege. During my baptism, my body was shaking, and the elders thought I was cold, but I repeatedly told them I was not. It baffled me how they were completely unable to see it was spiritual. Nonetheless, my grandmothers and other family members were there, which was very important to me. They asked if I wanted to say anything, and I sang a song, grateful to Yah for giving me the ability to sing. Then I went under, and the shaking stopped. Yet those around me looked confounded. This was a significant moment for me.

After some time, I would leave this church and start over on a new journey because my spiritual needs were no longer being met. I was able to see that the leaders of the church were not being led by the Spirit, and that was not where I wanted to be at all. Some would say I was backsliding, but I would say I needed to find myself and what God had for me specifically. However, the reality is that being in a world without guidance will bring sin, and sin leads to death.

Chapter 4: Adulting

I would later meet a kingdom helper who prayed with me while she was on a mission herself, staying at the local Salvation Army. It was of zero help to me, but she was a blessing. I then found another church and started my journey to become closer to the Holy Spirit. Again, it was some years, but short-lived because I had reached the threshold of what this place could provide for me. So many attacks in the spirit, and realizing I was not being covered, even though I was paying my tithes and being loyal to every service, every Bible study, every event. Sometimes at night, with my two young children on the bus, it was challenging, but I loved God so much that I made it possible with His strength.

The last chapter of my time in a physical church was interesting as I was asked to leave by the pastor after volunteering information that would, in some churches, be considered a confession. Yahweh led me to a house of prophets, which was very short-lived; however, it was possibly the most powerful experience my children and I had ever experienced. This was the first time I was able to actively use my gift of prophecy. Even my children were prophesying. Yahweh allowed me to see things more clearly in the spirit, and He continued to download information to me about what was to come not only for me but for all His people.

Then, it happened again. There was a blockage in movement with the Holy Spirit. The prophets were not in obedience to Yah's intention. They wanted to stay in the comfort of Egypt, but Yahweh was sending me into the wilderness for the second time, so I could finally enter my Promised Land. I had to leave and find my own way.

Being out in the world, alone without spiritual covering, without spiritual leaders, and without anyone to give me advice, was a daunting experience. At times, I didn't have anyone to pray for me, or with me. It was a scary time, but also a powerful one because it allowed me to use the power that God had given me. It allowed me to realize that His grace was with me and on me.

As a mother, it was important to me to raise my children according to the teachings of the Bible, "to raise a child in the way that they should go, so that when they grow older, they will not depart from it." In everything we did, we gave thanks, we prayed, and we sought after the Lord in a place of closeness. God had spoken to me about taking my children out of school and teaching them about our blackness, about being a true Hebrew, and about knowing who we are. His grace was sufficient for all our needs, and He supplied for us.

During this time, I truly knew and understood what it meant to have God's unmerited favour. I knew what it meant to receive when I didn't deserve to receive, even though I may have been outside of the Word of God. I received more than when I was paying tithes, when I was attending Bible study, or when I was at church service every day. It made no sense, and it was completely outside of what I was taught as a child of God growing up in the church. But I received His grace. My family was under His grace, and it was a truly wonderful and beautiful thing. It was an experience like no other.

God showed me His presence, His Holy Spirit, and His angels, and taught me how to be the child and woman of God that He has created me to be. He allowed me to teach that to my children. He showed me the secret things of the Word, reversed the doctrine that I had been taught in the church, and taught me the true gospel. He brought me to a place where I felt safe, secure, and comforted. I was able to take rest, even if it was just for a short while, but the rest was in Him. He hid me under the shadow of His wing. I was still being attacked in my dreams spiritually, but I was shielded. I had faith and used my sword, which is the Word, to fight back against the enemy because he's a liar and only comes to steal, kill, and destroy. I have the victory. Hallelujah

Manna holds a special significance for me. It's intriguing to realize that all this while, God has been providing for me in his unique way, teaching me not to worry and trust in Him completely. Unlike others, I never aspired to have the fanciest car or the biggest house. I knew that the things I needed and earned were beyond materialistic desires. And as I searched for what that would look like and how to achieve it, God provided His manner.

For me, His manner was having a sought-after home without paying anything for it, and I didn't have to work hard to earn it. I was able to travel and drive cars, second-hand or new, without worrying about the cost. My children and I always had food, clothing, and everything we needed, without having to work myself to the bone.
God's manner was like the manna in the book of Exodus, enough to last for the day. I didn't gather more than I needed, and God gave me the heart to be generous. He tested me to see how I could handle little so that I could manage my inheritance when it was time to receive it.

Despite all this, I sometimes felt like I wasn't doing enough, and that I should save more or own a house. I even tried looking for jobs, but nothing worked out. God had different plans for me, and He revealed to me that my singing voice was meant for Him. I realized that my voice could be used to heal the nations, and everything started to make sense.
God provides for us in His unique way, and we must trust in His provision. We should not worry about tomorrow because He will always provide for us. In your season of manna, remember that God did not bring you this far to leave you. He will always provide for you and your family in the name of Jesus.

Chapter 7: Dealing with the Enemy

Satan is always on the prowl, seeking whom he can devour. He wants to destroy everything that God has planned for your life. However, if you are in a place of protection and know that God loves and cares for you, you will be able to withstand the attacks of the enemy.

Even though you are under God's protection, the enemy can still find ways to get to you. He will use open doorways in your life, and he will use the people closest to you and your emotions to gain access. He is familiar with your weaknesses and will use them against you. The spirits of the enemy are familiar with your DNA, family members, and everything about you, and they will use this knowledge to their advantage.

If your weakness is the opposite sex, the enemy will use men and women of the world to distract you from your path. If your weakness is addiction, he will use drugs and alcohol to lure you away. Even your mindset can be used against you. That's why many people struggle with mental health issues. The enemy will try to convince you that God doesn't hear your prayers or that you are unworthy of His love.

However, you need to know that mental health is not a sign of weakness. but to gain understanding. The Bible says that a double-minded man is unstable in all his ways, but you must choose this day whom you will serve, and which report you will believe. The enemy will try to deceive you, but God has sent a message to you through this book to remind you that He hears your prayers and that you are not alone. The Bible says that there are more for you than there are against you.

Amid all the attacks, you have Yahweh Elohim, Father, Jesus (son), and the Holy Spirit. The Holy Spirit is your comforter and will guide you through the trials and tribulations of life. Do not grieve the Spirit but let it guide you.

The adversary will use all manner of things to attack you, including your family, your job, and even the animals in your house. He will try to steal from you, lie to you, and accuse you. He is the accuser of the brethren, and he will put you on trial, just as they put Jesus on trial.

Remember, God is not a God of religion but a God of relationship. He is a covenant-keeping God who will always keep His promises. Do not get entangled with religious spirits. Keep yourself in right standing with God, and you will always be the head and not the tail.

In conclusion, the adversary has no power over you. The battle has already been won. Stand firm in your faith, and the enemy will flee from you. God has already given you victory, and if you stay in right standing with Him, you will overcome every attack of the enemy.

God has a unique way of raising us up and allowing us to go through situations that may seem painful at the time. However, He uses those situations to infuse us with His power. As you read this book, I pray that you receive His power in your spirit even right now, that the Holy Spirit comes down upon you like fire from heaven and gives you the power you need to speak life into your situation, your circumstances, your family, your health, and your financial situation.

God sees it all, and He knows that your house will not crumble. You are a solid rock, and you will stand because you have put on the full armour of God and are prepared to stand on the day of battle. The battle has already been won, and you are a vessel used by God to show the enemy and his minions that the battle has been won.

God said that He will use foolish things to confound the wise, and those that think they are wise are about to be confounded by your power because you are the underdog. You are the one that doesn't look like it makes sense. Why would God use you? Why would you be the person of all people? It doesn't make sense. But that's the beauty of it all. God can use anyone willing to be used by Him.

I remember a time when a medical professional told me that I was delusional because I told him that I was going to be successful and very wealthy, despite not having a strong educational background or a job at the time. I was being assessed to be a guardian for my younger sister, and he didn't have the power to decide whether I would take care of her or not. He made it clear that he wouldn't choose me, but I knew that his opinion didn't matter. He didn't know the power of my Father in heaven, and he didn't understand the power that God had placed in me to speak things as they are in heaven.

Chapter 8: Gaining Power

The Bible says that there is life and death in the power of the tongue, and today, I choose life. When you know how to manifest, not new-age manifestation, but speaking life into your circumstances, being able to see the promises that God has before you, visualizing what He has shown you, and believing that it's true and standing firm in that thing, it will and shall come to pass. God has given you power as His chosen, His redeemed, and His remnant. You are needed here on Earth for a time such as this, and that's why the power was given to you for you to do the things that He needs you to do on Earth.

So be glad in this day that the Lord has made, and we shall rejoice and be glad in it. The power of God is your gift, and it's time to receive it fully. Embrace the power of God and allow it to flow through you, touching and changing lives wherever you go. May you continue to stand firm in your faith, knowing that God's power is working within you to accomplish great things for His Glory.

Chapter 9: Knowing Thyself

Do you know yourself? To know yourself is to know God. I went through a period of God changing my character and speaking to me about the person I once was, being needy of people. There's nothing wrong with needing people but being needy and needing are not the same thing. Being needy means that you need validation from people, and it's also a form of vanity.

Knowing yourself is to know God. The only way that I was able to be approved, tested, and purified was through the reading of the word. The more I understood the women of the Bible, the more I understood the characteristics of God, and the more I understood who Jesus was. This is a daily thing. It never stops, but you do get to a place where you know yourself. You know without a shadow of a doubt that you are a child of God. You know that He is your father. You know that whatever you choose to call yourself, a child of God, a Christian, this is your purpose in life, and you will not turn back from it.

Once you have accepted that, there is nothing the enemy can do to take you off that journey. It doesn't mean that attempts stop. It doesn't mean that nothing can go wrong. It simply means that you have arrived at a place in your mind, in your heart, in your soul, and spirit where you know who you are.

Know that the angels in heaven will rejoice when you receive this acknowledgement in your spirit. God himself will rejoice because now he doesn't have to prod or tell you, "My child, fix your crown." He doesn't have to tell you that you are the son or daughter of the one true living King, the King of kings. You belong to a Kingdom.

He doesn't have to tell you that everything in the world, everything on the earth, and everything above the earth, the firmament of the earth belongs to Him. So why see yourself in poverty? He doesn't have to tell you any of these things.

Through the wilderness, you may be in a place of loneliness. However, I'm here to tell you that you are not alone. You are never alone. You are surrounded by your angels filled with the Holy Spirit. You have people that have never even met you praying for you. Trust me, I've experienced it in a very personal way as an intercessor.

Chapter 9: Knowing Thyself

God will send you images of people or tell you situations and tell you to pray and sometimes even fast, and you've never met these people a day in your life. There are people even right now thanking God for you whom they have never met. Because of your Father in heaven, some things could have happened to you today or yesterday or even tomorrow that have been stopped in the spirit because God has sent out His prophets, His apostles, His ministers, and His intercessors to pray for you and send His angels ahead of you to clear the way so that you will not trip or stumble.

When you know yourself, you understand that you are not alone. You understand that you are the head and not the tail. You understand that you are blessed and highly favoured. You understand that you have everything that God has already provided for you for this day. It was already wrapped up in a little bow and prepared for you to receive. If you're struggling to find it, then read the word and ask the Holy Spirit to guide you on where to go and what to read.

God will speak to you and show you the things that you need to see. Knowing your Father is the key to knowing yourself and God's plan for your life. May you continue to grow in the knowledge of Him.

When order is restored in the wilderness season, it can feel like a breath of fresh air. We begin to settle in and feel at home. However, we must be careful not to rush back into the things of the world too quickly. We may be tempted to think that since the chaos has calmed down, we can go back to our everyday lives. But this is not the purpose of this part of the season.

God wants us to use this time to hear from Him without distraction. Just like Moses and Aaron were instructed to come up before God and leave the people to get directions and instructions on what to do next, we must also take this time to seek God's face, get on our knees, and cry out to Him. We should ask Him for instruction, direction, and revelation, especially if we are dreamers or prophets.

This is a time to be still, listen, pray, and seek God by fasting and prayer. It may be uncomfortable, but it is necessary for our spiritual growth and development. This is a season to trust in God, even when we cannot see the road ahead. We must learn to wait on Him and trust that His timing is perfect. With His guidance, we will come out of the wilderness season stronger, wiser, and more equipped for the next chapter of our lives.

There is nothing more beautiful in life than experiencing God's perfect peace. It is a peace that surpasses all understanding, and it can be found even during the stormiest of situations. When you have this peace, you can face any challenge that comes your way with confidence and grace.

God's peace has many different meanings and significance. It is a gift that can help you through all of life's situations. It is a tool that can be used to confound the wise, and it can help you navigate even the most difficult of circumstances with ease.

Sometimes, when you are going through a difficult season in life, you may feel like you are all alone. You may not have anyone to speak to, no job, and no family members to turn to, and your relationships may be strained. However, even in these situations, God's perfect peace is available to you.

Perfect peace looks like waking up without being upset with the things of the world. It means not getting easily frustrated with your children, even when they are not listening. It means not having road rage when you are stuck in traffic. It means not being miserable because the weather is not doing what you want it to do. It means not being frustrated because your finances do not look the way they are supposed to. It means not being offended because someone said something that doesn't make sense to you.

Having perfect peace does not mean that any of these things will not happen. It means that you have the calmness and wisdom to navigate through them with ease. When you can stay calm in adversity, you start to see the situation from another perspective, and you gain control over yourself. Self-control is also a gift from the Holy Spirit.

In this chapter, I pray that God allows you to experience his perfect peace, that surpasses all understanding, in all seasons, times, and situations. May you never go without any good thing, and may you always be able to navigate through life's challenges with grace and confidence. So be it.

Chapter 12: Under the Law

Living under the law of God is not always easy, but it is necessary for our spiritual growth and development. It is through the law that we can learn about God's expectations for us as His children and how we can live our lives following His will. When Jesus came, He made it clear that He did not come to abolish the law, but to fulfil it. This means that all the laws and rules that God has set for us are still important and relevant today. It may seem impossible to fulfil all of God's laws and expectations, but with His help, all things are possible.

God's law is not like man's law. Although we are also called to follow the laws of the land, the laws of God are meant to protect us and guide us towards righteousness. The people who create the laws of the land are placed there by God, and we must respect and pray for them.

It is important to understand that the system of the world is not the same as God's law. The system is created by Satan, while the law is created by God to protect and save us. In the Bible, the people of Israel initially did not have a king or a government, but they eventually asked God to give them a king. Saul was anointed as king, but he later had to step down because he was not following God's guidance. David was then anointed as king, and the monarchy continued through his bloodline.

In the same way, God anoints leaders to govern over each nation, and we must pray for them and respect their authority. However, there will come a time when the leaders of the world will not be the same as they are today. The leaders will be His judges. Prophets, Apostles, Preachers and Teachers – those whom God has given authority to judge His people.

Living under the law of God can be challenging, especially when dealing with legal situations that seem to go against us. But as children of God, we must remember that we are not alone, The Holy Spirit is your advocate. He will speak on your behalf and make you raise up with eagles swings out of the enemy's trap, so fear not. Seek His face in all things. Abba, Yahweh Sabaoth is there to help us, guide us, and protect us, so we should always trust Him and His guidance.

In conclusion, knowing and living under the law of God is crucial for our spiritual growth and development. It may seem difficult at times, but with God's help, all things are possible.

Dealing with witchcraft can be a challenging and intimidating experience. It is important to recognize the different forms that witchcraft can take. Witchcraft can be in the form of spells, potions, or even communicating with demonic spirits. It can also manifest in the form of controlling behaviours such as the spirit of Jezebel.

It is important to understand that witchcraft is not a myth, and warlocks and witches are very real today. Spiritual warfare is an essential part of one's spiritual journey and should not be underestimated. In my past, spiritual warfare was often only spoken about among the leaders of the church, but this is a lie. As a child of God, you have the power and grace to deal with witchcraft and other forms of spiritual attacks.

To identify witchcraft, you need to pay attention to controlling behaviours or any attempt to come between you and God. Witchcraft can also involve curses or negative talk about you, which goes against what God says about you. If someone is conjuring spells or demons over your life, you will feel it and experience negative things around you. Witchcraft can even be present in the systems, such as schools or workplaces.

Once you have identified witchcraft, it is important to attack it head-on and cut it at the root. Do not allow fear to stop you from breaking the curses of witchcraft over your life and that of your family. Speak to the demonic spirit at play, and if it is the spirit of Jezebel, tell her she has no authority and lose the hounds after her. The Bible says that any witch among you should not be left alive, not in the physical but in the spirit.

Remember that you have power, authority, and dominion to cast down every witch, warlock, spell, and demonic spirit. Speak these things into being as if they were and witness the hand of God move. Trust in God, and He will lead you to a place of peace and restoration, away from any form of witchcraft.

Chapter 14: Under God's Wing

As mankind, we often find ourselves in situations where we feel vulnerable, scared, or even helpless. It could be in the face of danger, adversity, or uncertainty. In such times, we look for a source of protection and comfort, something or someone to shield us from harm and guide us towards safety.

For many, that source is God. Throughout the Bible, we see numerous examples of people who trusted in God's protection and were saved from harm. Daniel, Shadrach, Meshach, and Abednego were all thrown into dangerous situations but were protected by God's hand. Mordecai's enemy had planned to hang him on a gallows, but instead, the tables were turned, and the enemy ended up being punished.

King David, too, knew the power of God's protection. He was described as a man after God's own heart because he felt God's heart, understood His character and emotions, and knew how to repent and turn away from wickedness. Despite facing numerous battles and wars, David was always victorious because he was hidden under God's wing.

David wrote Psalm 91, which describes the protection and refuge that God offers to those who trust in Him. It says that God will cover you with His feathers and under His wings, you will find refuge. His faithfulness will be your shield and rampart. You will not fear the terror of night or the arrow that flies by day, for God will be your refuge and your fortress.

Being under God's wing means having the assurance of His protection, guidance, and provision. It means being hidden in plain sight, yet safe from harm. It means being able to rest in the knowledge that God is watching over you and that no matter what happens, He is in control.

As we face the challenges of life, we can find comfort in knowing that we are under God's wing. We can trust in His protection, guidance, and provision. We can find rest and safety in Him, knowing that He is always with us and will never leave us or forsake us.

So, let us take refuge in the shadow of God's wing, find comfort in His protection, and rest in the assurance of His love. For under His wing, we are safe, and in His hands, we are protected.

Counterfeit relationships are a prevalent issue in our society today. These are relationships that are not sent from God and can hinder our blessings and progress in life. In this chapter, we will discuss the dangers of counterfeit relationships and how to identify them.

A counterfeit relationship is not in alignment with God's plan for our lives. It could be a relationship with someone who is not meant to be in our lives or a relationship that is based on physical attraction rather than true love. These relationships can be dangerous and harmful to our emotional, mental, and spiritual well-being.

In the story of Samson and Delilah, we see a perfect example of a counterfeit relationship. Delilah was not sent from God, and she was not supposed to be in Samson's life. Samson's strength was in his hair, which was given to him by God for a specific purpose. Delilah was close enough to Samson to be able to remove his hair and take away his strength. This shows how a counterfeit relationship can lead us away from our purpose and hinder us from achieving our goals.

My personal experience with a counterfeit relationship was with my son's father. I had prayed to God for a husband, but I had not asked for a man of God. I had a checklist of specific qualities I wanted, but I never considered the most important thing, which was for him to be from God. I lived in that relationship for years, not knowing it was a counterfeit one. It wasn't until I went through my wilderness experience that I realized it was not from God and was sent by the enemy to derail me from my purpose.

Counterfeit relationships can also be a hindrance to our blessings. If we are in a relationship that God did not bless, there will be constant strife, vexation, and no peace. Physical intimacy is not enough to hold a relationship together. If there is no love, there is no relationship with God. We need to be aware of these signs and leave the relationship alone.

It is also important to break these generational curses and put an end to the foolishness that the enemy continues to do in our bloodlines. If we continue to stay in counterfeit relationships, we are not teaching our children love but discord. We need to get out while we still can and teach our children the importance of Godly relationships.

In conclusion, counterfeit relationships are dangerous and can lead us away from our purpose and blessings. We need to pray for discernment and ask God to send us the right person who will be a blessing to our lives, being equally yolked for purpose. It is time to break these worldly behaviour patterns and put an end to the cycle of counterfeit relationships.

When most people think of Jezebel, they tend to associate her with harlotry, promiscuity, and other forms of sexual immorality. However, Jezebel was much more than that. She was a false prophetess who operated with a heavy spirit of control, pride, and witchcraft. She was a lying, deceitful woman who would stop at nothing to get what she wanted.

Jezebel was cunning and able to deceive people. As a spirit, she will hide behind other spirits and emotions so that the carrier will realise that they are carrying the Jezebel spirit in their lives. She deceives people to the point where they believe they should be in ungodly relationships, jobs, or experiences that were not in alignment with God's plan for their lives. This deception is a manifestation of the spirit of pride, which was an integral part of Jezebel's makeup.

Anything that goes against what God stands for is Jezebel. She doesn't care what she must do to get what she wants or what she believes in. Jezebel will deceive herself enough to even call herself a prophetess of God, even though she was worshipping Baal. It is important to understand what these demonic energies are and how they operate in our lives. We must not allow Jezebel to steal from us our purpose in life.

Jezebel's main goal was to kill the prophets of God. She tried to kill Elijah, but God protected him. We must learn how to identify the spirit of Jezebel in our lives and the people around us and kill that spirit. Just as we kill the spirit of witchcraft, we must cut it dead, sever ourselves from it, Repent of it, denounce it and renounce it, and remember to replace it with the blood of Jesus and God's will for our lives.

Jezebel is not just limited to women; men and even animals can carry this spirit. We must be vigilant and discerning in identifying this spirit in ourselves and others. We should ask God for discernment to recognize the Jezebel spirit and the strength to overcome it.

In conclusion, Jezebel is a dangerous spirit that manifests in various forms. She operates with a spirit of control, pride, sexual immorality, and witchcraft and was a lying, deceitful spirit. We must be vigilant and discerning in identifying this spirit in ourselves and others, By doing so, we overcome all demonic spirits.

The wilderness is a place where many people believe nothing good can come. It's a place of isolation, dryness, and loneliness. But what many fail to realize is that the wilderness is also a place where miracles happen. It's a place where God can show His power and do wonders in your life. However, it's important to pay attention to these miracles because they may come in different forms.

What is a miracle? Many believe that miracles are only big and spectacular events that are rare and hard to explain. However, miracles can be found in the everyday things that we often take for granted. Waking up every day, being healed from an illness, and even having food to eat are all miracles. God provides for us every day, and we should be grateful for the small miracles that He does in our lives.

The difference between being in your season of harvest and being in the wilderness is that in the season of harvest, miracles are abundant, while in the wilderness, they may be sporadic. However, God is still a miracle-working God, and He can perform miracles even in the most challenging times of our lives.

I experienced a miracle when my youngest daughter was born. At around five months old, I noticed that she was acting strange and took her to the hospital. The doctors said she was fine and sent us home, but the next day, they called and asked us to bring her back. They diagnosed her with Rickets, a disease caused by a lack of Vitamin D. Her bones were brittle, and she was malnourished. Meaning she needed the sun, which in the UK is hard to find.

I prayed and cried out to God for days as we spent time in the hospital doing tests on my child. It turned out that lacking Vitamin D, caused her bones to become brittle. The doctors gave her artificial calcium and Vitamin D drops, and it made a significant difference in her health. She was healed of Rickets, and the doctors were amazed.

But my miracle didn't end there, later Yahweh Jireh would provide us with the sun needed to nourish our melanated skin in the tropical environment He indented for his people. Glory to God.

While in the hospital, I was in spiritual warfare because of the heavy witchcraft and demonic control in these places. However, the Holy Spirit guided me and told me that my child would be healed. I was on my face in that hospital room, day and night, praying and reading the word on my phone. God took a situation where the enemy tried to take my child's life and made her well. He showed me signs, and then He created His wonders.

The doctors had told me that my daughter's body would be bent, her legs would be bent, and she would be weak and brittle. However, none of those things happened. When we got a second opinion, they said that my child was perfectly healthy and would grow up normally. It was all because of God's miracle-working power.

In conclusion, God still performs miracles today, even in the wilderness. We just must pay attention and believe that He can do the impossible. God is the God of Abraham, Isaac, and Jacob, and He is still the same yesterday, today, and forever.

Chapter 18: Lest You Die

When God speaks, it's important to listen and follow his directions. Every step is crucial, and there's no room for hesitation. It's a matter of life and death. This is something I learned first-hand.

A few months into the Covid pandemic, I had just given birth to a beautiful baby girl. I was feeling overwhelmed and desperate for a change of scenery. I longed for the warmth of the sun and the sand between my toes. I had dreamt about this moment throughout my pregnancy, imagining drinking fresh coconut water and eating fresh fruit while soaking up the sun on a Jamaican beach.

But there I was, stuck in a dreary apartment in London, caring for my newborn and teens. It was far from the dream I had envisioned.

Then, my child got sick. I spent a long time in the hospital, feeling sad and helpless. But that was just the beginning of my troubles.

I found myself facing the system. Social services accused me of malnourishing my child because I was plant-based and didn't feed her cow's milk or other animal products. They told me that the sea moss I was giving her, which has 92 of the 102 minerals that the body needs, was giving her too much iodine.

I knew that wasn't true. The sea moss was what had kept my child alive. But they were determined to trap me.

They threatened me with their laws and strategic plans. They told me that if I were to be reported again, they would take me to court and remove my children from me. But I wasn't afraid. I was fed up with all the enemies' plans to break up my anointed family, created and put together by God for a time such as this.

Amid my struggles, God was devising a plan for my escape. He was giving me directions, and I knew that I needed to take every step very seriously, lest I die.

If God tells you to pack your bags, you pack your bags. You don't need to know where you're going. If he tells you to clean your house, you clean your house. If he tells you to bathe, you bathe. You don't know what might happen, who might knock on your door, or what might turn up.

Take every instruction seriously, without hesitation. Your life may depend on it.

I learned this the hard way in the past. But I also learned that God is always with us, even in our darkest moments. He will guide us and protect us if we trust and follow him.

Chapter 19: All Things Are Possible

It's easy to get bogged down by the challenges we face in life, whether they're financial, health-related, or personal. When things get tough, it's easy to forget that we serve a God who is bigger than any obstacle we may face. In times of struggle, it's important to remember that all things are possible with God.

In Mark 10:27, Jesus tells his disciples, "With man, this is impossible, but not with God; all things are possible with God." This verse is a powerful reminder that when we put our trust in God, there is nothing that He cannot do for us. No obstacle is too big, no challenge too great, and no problem too complex for our God.

It's important to approach God with childlike faith, just as Jesus said in Matthew 18:3: "Truly I tell you, unless you change and become like little children, you will never enter the kingdom of heaven." Children believe that anything is possible, and that's the kind of faith that God wants us to have. He wants us to trust in Him completely, without trying to figure everything out ourselves.

When we put our trust in God, we tap into His power and His ability to do the impossible. We don't have to rely on our strength or our understanding; we can simply trust that God will provide for us and make a way where there seems to be no way.

So today, no matter what you may be facing, remember that all things are possible with God. Ask Him to help you approach life with childlike faith, and to trust in Him completely. He will come through for you in ways that you could never imagine, and He will show you that with Him, all things are truly possible.

In a world filled with distractions and chaos, it's easy to feel lost and unsure about our purpose. We may find ourselves asking, "What am I doing here?" or "What's the point of all this?" However, the answer lies in seeking God and His will for our lives.

Jesus said, "Ask, and it will be given to you; seek, and you will find; knock, and it will be opened to you" (Matthew 7:7). When we come to God with a sincere heart and ask for guidance, He promises to answer us. He may not always answer in the way we expect or on our timetable, but we can trust that He will answer.

Sometimes, when we feel like we're not hearing anything from God, it can be helpful to seek the counsel of others. We can ask for prayer and support from fellow believers, or we can seek out wise and trusted mentors to help guide us.

Another way to gain clarity is through fasting. Fasting is not just about receiving something from God; it's also about surrendering our desires and allowing Him to speak to us more clearly. By turning down our plates and silencing our flesh, we create space to hear the Holy Spirit more clearly.

Meditation is also a powerful tool for seeking God's guidance. We can meditate on His word and allow Him to speak to us through Scripture. As we focus on His truth, we will gain clarity and direction for our lives.

God is not a man that He should lie, He has promised that if we seek Him, we will find Him (Jeremiah 29:13). He wants us to seek Him with all our hearts and to prioritize His kingdom above all else. When we do this, He promises to add all the other things we need to our lives (Matthew 6:33).

We can seek God in many ways, from studying His word to listening for His voice in dreams and visions. He is our spiritual adviser, financial adviser, and relationship adviser. He is everything we need, and when we seek Him, we will find Him.

So let us make seeking God a priority in our lives, and trust that He will guide us every step of the way. As we seek, we will find not only what we are looking for, but also so much more than we could ever imagine.

Studying the Word of God is crucial for our spiritual growth and development. It is through studying that we gain knowledge, wisdom, and understanding of God's will and purpose for our lives. In 2 Timothy 2:15, the Bible tells us to "study to show yourself approved unto God, a workman that needed not to be ashamed, rightly dividing the word of truth."

When we study the Word of God, we are showing our commitment to God and our desire to know Him more deeply. We are also equipping ourselves with the tools we need to navigate the challenges and trials that we may face in life. Through the Scriptures, we can gain strength, guidance, and direction for our lives.
It is important to approach studying the Word with the right mindset. We should not study simply to gain knowledge or to impress others with our understanding of the Scriptures. Instead, we should study with a humble and teachable heart, seeking to hear from God and align ourselves with His will.

Studying the Word can take many forms. It can involve reading, meditating, memorizing, and discussing the Scriptures with others. It can also involve studying the historical and cultural context in which the Scriptures were written, as well as studying the original languages in which they were written.

As we study the Word, we should also be open to the leading of the Holy Spirit. The Spirit can give us insight and understanding that we might not gain through our efforts alone. We should also be willing to allow the Word to challenge us and transform us, shaping us into the people that God desires us to be.

Ultimately, studying the Word is about building a relationship with God. It is about seeking to know Him more deeply and aligning our lives with His will. As we do so, we can be confident that we are pleasing Him and that we are preparing ourselves for the work that He has called us to do. So let us all commit to studying the Word of God, seeking to show ourselves approved unto Him.

Being called by God is an honour and a privilege. As a prophet, your calling is unique and special. It is not something that can be obtained through man's approval or ordination but through God's divine appointment.

A true prophet in God's eyes is dedicated to seeking and serving God and has a deep understanding of His Word. This understanding is gained through study, prayer, and a willingness to be led by the Holy Spirit.

A prophet's role is to speak the truth of God's Word, to edify, exhort, and comfort the church. They are called to warn of impending judgment, to call people to repentance, and to share the good news of salvation.

However, being a prophet is not always easy. Prophets are often misunderstood, rejected, and even persecuted for speaking the truth. They may face opposition from those who do not want to hear what they have to say, or from those who are afraid of change.

But despite the challenges, a true prophet remains faithful to God's call on their life. They continue to speak the truth in love, trusting in God's strength to sustain them.

One of the key characteristics of a true prophet is humility. They recognize that their gift is not their own, but a gift from God and that they are simply a vessel through which God speaks. They do not seek their glory or fame, but rather the glory of God.

Another characteristic of a true prophet is a deep love for God's people. They are burdened for the souls of those around them and are willing to go to great lengths to see them come to salvation and live a life of obedience to God.

To be a true prophet, you must also be willing to be corrected and to receive guidance from other prophets and spiritual leaders. No prophet is an island, and it is important to have a community of believers who can speak into your life and help you stay accountable to God's call.

In conclusion, being a true prophet in God's eyes requires dedication, humility, and a deep love for God and His people. It is a high calling that comes with great responsibility, but also great reward. So, if you believe that God has called you to be a Prophet in His eyes. I pray you to walk in your purpose with His perfect peace.

Forgiveness is a powerful tool that can heal even the deepest of wounds. It can bring peace to those who have been hurt and release those who have caused pain from the burden of guilt. It's a beautiful thing to see the transformative power of forgiveness in action.

But forgiveness is not always easy. It requires us to let go of our anger, resentment, and desire for revenge. It asks us to move beyond our pain and extend compassion to those who have hurt us. Forgiveness is not weakness, nor is it condoning the actions of others. It's a conscious choice to release ourselves from the grip of negative emotions and allow healing to take place.

One of the most difficult forms of forgiveness is self-forgiveness. It's easy to beat ourselves up over past mistakes and dwell on our failures. But dwelling on our shortcomings only keeps us stuck in a cycle of self-blame and prevents us from moving forward. We must learn to forgive ourselves for our mistakes and trust that we have learned from them.

Forgiveness is also an essential component of healthy relationships. When we hold onto grudges and resentments, it creates a toxic environment that can destroy even the strongest of bonds. Learning to forgive our loved ones, even when they have hurt us, can strengthen our relationships and bring us closer together. It requires humility, vulnerability, and a willingness to let go of our ego.

In some cases, forgiveness may not seem possible or appropriate. In situations where we have been abused or traumatised, forgiveness can be a complex process that may require professional help. It's important to prioritise our safety and well-being and seek support from those who can help us navigate the process of healing and forgiveness. Knowing Yahweh Rafa is our healer He will provide rest.

Ultimately, forgiveness is a choice that we make for ourselves. It's a decision to let go of the past and move forward with an open heart. It's a way to break free from the chains of resentment and anger and experience the freedom and peace that comes with forgiveness. When we choose forgiveness, we choose to love, and that is God's plan for His people.

Chapter 24: Are We There Yet?

As I sat in my prayer closet, speaking with Abba, I couldn't help but wonder, "Are we there yet?" It was a question that had been lingering in my mind for quite some time. I had been on this journey for what felt like ages, and I was so close to achieving my dreams, yet it still seemed like there was so much more to do.

I knew that I had come a long way, and had already accomplished so much, but I couldn't help feeling like there was still so much left to do. It was like being in a car on a long road trip with no end in sight, and I was that annoying kid in the back seat constantly asking, "Are we there yet?"

I had put in countless hours, days, weeks, and months of hard work, and I could see the fruits of my labour beginning to blossom. But it was frustrating because I knew that I wasn't quite there yet. I was in that limbo between almost reaching my goal and achieving it.

I thought about the Israelites in the wilderness, and how they had to go through various tests and trials before they could reach the Promised Land. It was a long and arduous journey, but they persevered because they trusted God's plan.
Similarly, in our own lives, we must learn to trust in God's plan and timing. We may feel like we are ready to receive our blessings and rewards, but God may still have a few more things for us to do before we can fully receive them.

Giving is one of the things that God requires of us, and it's a big one. Giving freely and generously is an important part of our journey, and it's something that we must do if we want to receive the blessings that God has in store for us.
As I sat there, pondering all of this, I realized that perhaps this limbo that I was in was just an interlude. Maybe it was just a brief pause in my journey, a time to reflect, regroup, and prepare for the next phase of my journey.

I decided to use this time to continue to work hard, to pray, to fast, and to give freely. I knew that in due time, God would take me to where I needed to be, and I would finally be able to say, "Yes, we are there."

The world is filled with beautiful places, but sometimes even amid breathtaking scenery, one can feel incredibly alone. It's important to remember that despite the isolation, angels are watching over you, people praying for you, and things around you God has provided for your care.

Perhaps you've had to let go of family members or close friends or ended a counterfeit relationship. But if you trust in God, He will replace those individuals with people who are meant to be in your life. These are the ones who are anointed to be around you because you are called and chosen for a purpose. Anyone in your life must be able to handle the responsibilities of your calling and understand that it should never be taken for granted.

It's possible to experience two seasons at once in different areas of your life. You could be blessed financially while still struggling with relationships. This can make you feel alone, especially if you are surrounded by people who don't understand your situation. That's why it's important to give God room to bring people into your life who will congratulate you, pray for you, fast with you, and stand with you in all seasons.

So even when you're in a beautiful place, it's possible to feel lonely. But remember that God is always with you and will provide the right people to support you. Trust in His timing and believe that your true tribe is on its way.

At this point in your journey, everything should be starting to make sense. God has given you all the tools and directions you need, and now it's time for you to put them in place. It feels good to see everything come together as God has promised, and he continues to download information to you daily.

The one certain thing is that you know he is with you and that you are not alone. You start to notice the signs of the things God has done in your life and you create biblical altars to Yahweh Elohim, like an Ebenezer stone. My advice during this part of your wilderness journey is to give thanks.

Give thanks to God for everything that has brought you through. If you look back and see how far you've come, you've achieved so much in this season, and you deserve to give God the praise and give yourself a pat on the back. Congratulations! This is the hardest season of your life, and you've accomplished so much because of the grace and favour of God in your life.

Now, you are ready to take on the final battle, the final breakthrough prayer and fasting, the final pieces to your puzzle that need to be added to you so that you can go forth and do the work that your father has sent you to do. You can finally step into your purpose and fulfil the destiny God has planned for you. Hallelujah, glory to God!

Going through a wilderness season is never easy, but it can be particularly challenging when you have family members who are also navigating this difficult time with you. It can be tough to balance your personal growth and renewal with the needs and concerns of your loved ones, especially if they do not share your faith or beliefs.

As you move through the wilderness, it's essential to communicate with your family members and ensure that they understand what's happening and what God is telling you to do. You must build trust with them so that they feel confident in following your lead, even if it means making significant changes in their lives.

If there are family members who do not believe or do not want to follow the path that God has set for them, it's essential to continue to pray for them and trust that God will work in their lives in His own time. You cannot force anyone to believe or follow God's plan, but you can lead by example and show them the power of faith and obedience.

Having a family that prays together and supports one another through the wilderness season can be a tremendous source of strength and comfort. It's crucial to prioritize your family and put God first in your household, creating a foundation of love and faith that will carry you through even the toughest times.

However, it's important to be aware that the enemy will do everything in his power to try to break apart your family and undermine your faith. Stay vigilant and watchful, closing every door and bridge that could allow the enemy to enter your home and cause division. Pray together, repent when necessary, and keep your eyes fixed on God's promises.

Ultimately, as you and your family move through the wilderness, you must remain on one accord and at peace. Trust in God's plan for your lives and hold fast to the knowledge that He is with you every step of the way, guiding and supporting you as you navigate this challenging season together.

Breaking curses and covenants can be one of the most important stages in your spiritual journey. It is a process that requires your full attention, dedication, and faith. Curses and covenants are things that give the enemy access to your life. They are like chains that bind you to the past, and they make it difficult for you to move forward.

To break these curses and covenants, you must first understand that spiritual warfare is like a court in procession. God's law is the law of the spiritual, and even the enemy and his minions must adhere to the law. The Holy Spirit is your counsellor, and He speaks on your behalf. The angels fight on your behalf, Jesus intercedes on your behalf, and the Father makes all the final decisions when there are ungodly covenants in your life.

Generational curses are hard to break. You may have fasted, prayed, been through deliverance multiple times, been anointed with every type of oil, cried out to God, given up everything, given charity, and still, the enemy is trying to get into your household. This is because ungodly covenants and curses have not yet been truly broken.

Fasting is one of the first steps to breaking curses and covenants. Fast for three days from sunup to sundown, where you eat nothing and only drink water. If you are seasoned in fasting, you can do a dry fast. The purpose of fasting is to quiet your flesh and hear from the Lord.

HOW TO BREAK DEMONIC
Covenants & Curses

1. Read the entire book on breaking curses and covenants. The book recommended is "Prayers that Rout Demons" by John Eckhardt. You need to read every word in the book from beginning to end, including the Scriptures that are attached to them. The Bible says to speak and shame the devil. You need to speak these things out loud.

2. Detach yourself from any distractions around you, such as social media, your phone, and people who might have ungodly spirits. This is not part of the fast, but it is advice given to you to clear the noise.

3. Clear out anything in your home that could be an abomination to God, such as anything that looks like it could be any form of idle or idol worship. Remove it, get rid of it, and throw it away. If you have things from past relationships, those are the kind of things that you can donate depending on your season. God may be trying to simplify your life and get rid of most of your things to prepare you for what is to come.

Baal, Ashtoreth, and Molech were ancient deities worshipped by various pagan cultures. Baal is associated with storms and fertility (idle worship) while Ashtoreth was the goddess of love and war. Molech was a god associated with child sacrifice. In the Old Testament, the worship of these gods was often condemned by the prophets (and still is) as idolatry and a betrayal of the one true God. Remember Repent Renounce Replace.
-CHARLENE

During the fast, you will read the prayers of the book. You can download this book via the link provided, it will redirect you to purchase on amazon. You can get the PDF version once you've paid for the audible book. Once you have completed this, you want to make sure that anything that you feel may have been missed on your bloodline is covered. The book covers everything, but there are specific things that you may need to repent for.

Breaking curses and covenants is a process that requires your full attention, dedication, and faith. It is not something that you can do overnight, but with patience and persistence, you can break free from the chains of the past and move forward into a new season of your life. Remember that the Holy Spirit is your counsellor, and He will guide you through this process. Trust in God, and He will set you free.

After completing the three-day fast and reading the entire book of prayers,

It is important to understand that breaking covenants and curses is not a one-time event. It is a process that may require multiple sessions of prayer and fasting. It may also require seeking the help of a spiritual leader or counsellor who can guide you through the process.

During the prayer and breaking process, it is important to repent for any sins or transgressions that may have contributed to the covenants and curses. This may include sins committed by ancestors or family members that have been passed down through the bloodline.

It is also important to renounce any ties or connections to occult or witchcraft practices, as these can open doors to demonic activity and curses.

Finally, it is important to fill the void by replacing the ungodly covenants and curses with the power of the Holy Spirit. Asking God to enter you as His vessel. Restoring the covenant that your Father has made with you through Abraham Issac and Jacob. The only covenant you should agree with.

Remember, breaking covenants and curses is a powerful spiritual act that can lead to freedom and victory in your life. It may not be easy, but with the help of the Holy Spirit and a strong support system, it is possible to break free from the chains of generational curses and live a life of abundance and blessings.

Fasting and prayer are two spiritual disciplines that go hand in hand. Fasting is more about quieting the flesh and allowing yourself to be still enough to hear from God. It is a way to put your spirit at the forefront, where it should be always so that you can hear from God.

If you are called, chosen, or part of the five-fold ministry, you need to fast regularly. Fasting helps you to gain direction, guidance, and understanding from the Father.

Prayer, on the other hand, is a relationship. It is a conversation and communication with God. It should be a daily, hourly, moment-by-moment thing, just like having a conversation with your spouse or children.

In your prayer life, ask God for everything, from blessings on your food to what to wear, whom to talk to, and what job to take. Always pray that His will be done in your life.

As you continue to fast and pray, you will reach a point where you are asking for the things that God wants for you, rather than worldly desires. You will break down strongholds, get rid of ungodly covenants, and be able to hear God's voice more clearly.

Fasting and prayer should become a part of your lifestyle, not just a one-time thing. As you deepen your relationship with God, your desire to fast and pray will grow. And when you hear from Him, you will know that it is His voice speaking to you.

So, I encourage you to fast regularly and pray continually, knowing that as you draw closer to God, He will reveal His plans and purposes for your life. May your relationship with the Father become the most important relationship in your life. In Jesus' name, so be it.

In the wilderness, when we feel lost and alone, it can be easy to forget the power of praise and worship. But in truth, it is one of the most valuable tools we have to connect with our Creator and find strength and hope in difficult times.

Praising God is about recognising His greatness and giving Him all the honour, praise, and glory, He deserves. When we praise Him, we acknowledge everything He has done for us and in everything, He is worthy of our praise.

Worship, on the other hand, is about singing praises, lifting our voices, and making a joyful noise. It's about expressing our love and gratitude to God in a way that connects us to Him and strengthens our faith.

There are countless ways to worship, from singing and dancing to writing and even silent meditation. The important thing is that we give our worship and praise to God and Jesus simultaneously, recognizing their unity and the power of their love and grace in our lives.

Sometimes we may have to use wisdom in the type of worship we choose, especially depending on our surroundings and the people we are with. But the most important thing is to never deny our Father, the one who created us and sent us on our journey through the wilderness.

We can learn from the mistakes of Peter, who denied Jesus three times but was still a disciple and ambassador for Him. Even if we make mistakes, we can still stand strong in our faith and lift God's name in all areas of our lives.

Praise and worship should never become cliche or routine. They are powerful tools that can transform our lives and bring us closer to God. When we give our all-in worship and praise, we tap into the power of prayer and open ourselves up to the strength and guidance of our Creator.

In the wilderness, it can be easy to feel lost and alone, but when we turn to praise and worship, we find the hope and strength we need to keep moving forward. So let us lift our voices and hearts in praise and worship, and trust in the power of Yah to guide us through even the toughest times and of course to silence the enemy.

As a believer, it's essential to develop the ability to hear God's voice, especially when you're seeking answers or direction. Whether you're praying, fasting, worshipping, or praising, it's crucial to listen for the voice of God. But how can you hear Him?

God speaks to us in many ways, and we need to pay attention to the signs. He may speak to us through visions, dreams, nature, friends, strangers, children, numbers, and colours. Sometimes, He may even speak audibly, especially if you have the gift of prophecy.

If you speak in tongues, the Holy Spirit may give you the gift of interpretation, allowing you to hear God's voice directly. If you're new to the faith, pay attention to the signs. It could be a letter or an email, and a word or a number may stick out to you, prompting you to do some research.

When you hear God's voice audibly, it brings peace, and it may sound like someone speaking next to you. His voice is still and quiet, but He wants you to hear what He has to say. If you hear from the Father in any way, shape, or form, it's essential to take notes and write everything down in a journal. Include the time and date, your prayers, requests, and petitions, so you have a reference to go back to.

Sometimes, God answers our prayers in unexpected ways, and having a reference allows us to see how He has blessed us and those around us. There may also be times when He wakes you up in the middle of the night to pray or intercede for others.

If you have the gift of intercession, you may experience seasons of rest, but it's crucial to spend time with the Father to refresh and hear His voice. This way, you can discern His voice from the enemy's tricks. Remember that if it feels peaceful, it's from God. So, be patient and wait for His answers, and trust in His Ruach.

Chapter 32: Whom Can I Trust?

As you continue your wilderness journey, you will become increasingly sensitive to everything happening around you. You will be alert to the monitoring spirits, witchcraft, demonic spirits, idol worship, disobedience, and ungodly covenants. Your Father will point out all these things to you so that you can distance yourself from anything or anyone that will hold you back from your blessings.

At this point, you may wonder whom you can trust. There are people that God will place in your life, your true tribe, that you can trust. However, the average person that you had in your life while living in the world, even if you had the Holy Spirit with you, you cannot trust anymore.

So, what does this mean for you? Does it mean that you no longer speak to people because you know you can't trust them? Well, it depends on what your Father has told you. If He has instructed you to stay in and completely quiet yourself away from the world, then you shouldn't be speaking to anybody apart from those in your house going through this with you. But if He has told you, it's time to go out and be tested, then you will have the freedom to speak to certain people, but there will be limits to it.

You will be limited to whom you can speak to, how you can speak to them, and what you can say. Your Father may have told you a lot of things about your future, such as your God-ordained spouse, the investments He wants you to make, where you are going to move to, where your promised land is, the children He has promised you, and more. He will tell you to keep these things quiet, protect your blessings, breakthrough, and promise.

In short, the only people you can trust with your promises are those whom God has allowed being with you during the entire wilderness season. If you still have somebody in your life that God has not permitted at this stage, you will not pass over to the other side. You will not reach the promised land unless you are quick to remove anything that God did not permit you to have at this stage.

So, trust in God and His leading. He will guide you to the right people at the right time. Stay sensitive to His voice and continue to obey His instructions. Shalom.

As you approach the end of your journey, you may start to wonder if there is anything else you need to do or say. You may even feel like you need to pray more, but at this stage, the most important thing for you to do is to be still. Stand strong and firm in the word, everything that God has told you and everything that He has taught you. Remember every lesson you have learned and all the miracles that He has provided for you along the way.

It can be easy to become weary, especially if you feel like you are waiting for something to happen so that you can move to the next stage of your journey. Your physical surroundings may still resemble a wilderness but remember that everything happens in the spirit before it happens in the natural. In your mind and mentality, you are already in your promised land. This is even more reason for you to be still and wait patiently for the natural to catch up with the spiritual.

Trust that God is in control and that His plans for you are good. He is faithful and will never leave you nor forsake you. So be still and know that He is God. Rest in His presence and find peace in the knowledge that He is with you every step of the way. Cover yourself in the blood of Jesus and put on your heavenly armour and stand firm. Ephesians 6:10.

As you journey towards your promised land, your faith will be tested. You may be asked by God to do things that seem illogical, uncomfortable or unpopular with the world around you. You may be ridiculed or called crazy but remember that obedience to God is better than sacrifice 1 Samual 15:22. The testing of your faith is necessary to ensure that you are truly ready to fulfil the purpose that God has for you.

To pass these tests, you must be able to walk in faith and trust that God will provide for you. You must stand firm on the words that God has given you and do everything that he asks of you. Do not be swayed by the opinions or advice of others but focus solely on what God is telling you to do.

It is important to remember that many may claim to know God but do not truly have a relationship with Him. Do not allow yourself to be led astray by those who do not have a genuine connection with God.

As you face these tests, stay rooted in your faith and seek guidance through prayer and time spent in God's word. Trust that God has a plan for you and that he will see you through every trial and tribulation.

In the end, the testing of your faith will make you stronger and better equipped to fulfil God's purpose for your life. So, hold on, stay steadfast and let your faith be tested by the one who knows you best - your heavenly Father.

Chapter 35: Stand On The Word

In this chapter, the importance of standing on God's promises is emphasized. When going through a wilderness season, it can be easy to lose hope and doubt God's plan for your life.

However, it is crucial to remember that God's word is true, and his promises will come to pass. Believing and standing firm in his promises are key to getting through the tough times and coming out stronger on the other side.

Chapter 36: Decree & Declare

In this chapter, the focus is on speaking life into every situation and circumstance. Decreeing and declaring is a bold and powerful act that lets the enemy know that you are taking back everything that he has stolen. By speaking God's promises into existence, you are claiming what is rightfully yours and taking hold of your inheritance.

It is important to remember that everything happens first in the spiritual realm before manifesting in the physical world, so speaking life and truth is crucial in seeing change and transformation in your life. You have the power in your tongue. Proverbs 18:21-21

During the wilderness season, changes, signs, and wonders can occur in your life. These three things do not happen in any particular order, but they are significant and may come towards the end of the season. The season tests and proves you, removes things that needed to be removed and helps you grow closer to God. As a result, God can trust you with greater things for His glory.

Some of the changes you may notice during this season are an increase in patience, giving, and the fruits of the Spirit. Additionally, you may see an increase in the gifts of the Spirit, such as prophecy, healing, and speaking in tongues. Even if you have never prophesied or spoken in tongues before, God can use this season to equip you with the necessary gifts for your mission as His ambassador for the kingdom.

In my personal experience, I had already received many spiritual gifts, but I had never spoken in tongues. However, through the prompting of the Holy Spirit, I was able to speak in tongues as if I had been doing it my entire life. Look out for the spiritual gifts, changes, signs, and wonders that may occur in your life during this season. Remember to trust in God's plan and purpose for your life and use these gifts and experiences to glorify God. Shalom

In this chapter, we will explore the benefits of decluttering your life. When we talk about decluttering, we are referring to getting rid of anything that is not necessary or useful in our lives. This could be physical items such as clothes, shoes, or household items, but it can also include relationships, activities, and even thoughts. Firstly, decluttering can help you to learn contentment. We live in a society that tells us that we need to have more, do more, and be more to be happy. However, the truth is that less is often more. God's ways are not our ways. When we declutter our lives, we realise that we don't need the things of the world to be happy and content. We learn to be content with what God provides.

Secondly, decluttering can bring peace and order to our lives. When we have too much stuff, it can feel overwhelming and chaotic. We spend so much time trying to organize and manage the belongings that we forget to enjoy life. By decluttering, we create more space and order in our homes and our minds. We feel more in control of our lives and less stressed.

Thirdly, decluttering can help us to let go of the past. We often hold onto things that remind us of a person, a place, or a time in our lives. However, holding onto these things can prevent us from moving forward and embracing new experiences. By decluttering, we let go of the past and create space for new opportunities and memories.

Finally, decluttering prepares us for the purpose. As the world changes and we face new challenges, it's important to be adaptable and flexible. By decluttering, we learn to let go of what is not necessary and focus on what is truly important. We become more resourceful and prepared for whatever the future may bring.
In conclusion, decluttering is not just about getting rid of physical items. It's about finding contentment in simplicity. It's about letting go of the past and preparing for the future. So, take some time to declutter your life and enjoy the many benefits that come with it.

Chapter 39: Out Of The Miry Clay

The journey through life can be likened to a walk through a muddy field. Sometimes we find ourselves stuck in the mire, sinking deeper with each step we take. It's a place of struggle, pain, and discomfort. But just as the mud can be washed away, so too can we be lifted out of the mire.

When we have endured the struggles, the tests, and the obstacles, and have finally achieved the thing we sought after, it's as if we are lifted out of the mud and placed on solid ground. The Holy Spirit lets us know that we have climbed every wall, jumped over every hurdle, and passed every test. We have done everything possible to get through our season, and we are now out of the miry clay.

This is a time for celebration and gratitude. We should be pleased with ourselves and those in our circle who have supported us along the way. We should also take this opportunity to reflect on the journey that brought us here. What did we learn? How did we grow? What did we overcome?

It's easy to become weary in the mire, to feel like we will never escape its grip. But we must hold on to the promise that our breakthrough is coming. It's not even coming anymore because it's already been done. It's just loading, and we must have faith and patience for it to arrive.

So, if you find yourself in the mire, know that it's not a permanent place. Keep pushing forward, keep climbing, keep jumping, and keep passing those tests. And when you finally find yourself out of the mud, take a deep breath, feel the solid ground beneath your feet, and give thanks for the journey that brought you to your promises. Psalm 40

Congratulations!

You have made it to the other side of the wilderness, and your inheritance is waiting for you. The journey has been long, but the reward is sweet and filled with milk and honey, just as the scriptures say in Exodus 3:8. I am thrilled that we have made it to this stage together. This is the ultimate celebration!

However, this is not the end of the road. It's just the beginning of a wonderful journey as Yahweh's ambassador. He needs you to go out and do the work He has for you, wherever and whenever He sends you.

You may have to go into areas of the world that you have previously avoided or be around worldly people, but don't worry, you've got this. You have all the tools you need, and you've passed every test. There is no trick the enemy has that you have not seen. They all tend to be similar because he is not more powerful than your Father in Heaven.

Now it's time to be filled with good fruit after giving your first fruits to God. But most importantly, enjoy the journey! Smile, be glad, and revel in your blessings. You have made it through the trials and tribulations, and now it's time to enjoy the fruits of your labour.

One day, I hope to see you on the field or hear about the wonderful things God has you doing. Or maybe I will see or feel you in the spirit. Whatever it may look like for you, I know that God is with you, and you are blessed.

As you continue this amazing journey, I pray that you do so with the joy of the kingdom and that nothing stands in your way. You go forth in the mighty name of Jesus and may blessings and shalom be upon you all. So be it.

Thank you!

As God's prophet, I take my work very seriously. I wrote this book for those that need guidance navigating their wilderness season. I personally know the difficulties of doing it alone. I pray my words have given you a Spiritual Impartation to better prepare you. Making way for Yahweh Elohom to activate great exploits in your life.

Please use the links provided if you need more help, I give free support and prayer requests are also welcome. Please recommend this eBook to a friend, follow me on Instagram and subscribe to my Youtube channel.

I have Prophetic videos on both platforms. Please like and share.

Seed offerings are welcome if you feel led by the Spirit, you can donate via CashApp £CharleneNatasha. Blessings and Shalom.

Do You Need More Help?

Schedule a Free Call

Be Transformed By The Wilderness
And Make A Way For Yah.
A voice of one calling: 'In the wilderness prepare the way of
Yahweh, make straight in the desert a highway for Elohim.
Isaiah 40:3

Charlene Natasha Rebecca Francis

WILDERNESS
notes

WILDERNESS
notes

WILDERNESS
notes

WILDERNESS
notes

WILDERNESS
notes

WILDERNESS
notes

WILDERNESS
notes

WILDERNESS
notes

WILDERNESS
notes

WILDERNESS
notes

WILDERNESS
notes

WILDERNESS

notes

WILDERNESS
notes

WILDERNESS
notes

WILDERNESS
notes